CHRISTIANITY AND THE
MODERN WORLD VIEW

CHRISTIANITY
AND THE MODERN
WORLD VIEW

By

H. A. HODGES

*Professor of Philosophy
in the University of Reading*

LONDON

S·P·C·K

1962

First published 1949
by S.C.M. Press
Second edition 1962
by S.P.C.K.
Holy Trinity Church
Marylebone Road
London N.W.1

Made and printed in Great Britain by
William Clowes and Sons, Limited, London and Beccles

NOTE: This book originally appeared as Supplements
to the *Christian News-Letter*, and thanks are due to the
Editor for permission to reprint.

Contents

Preface

THE chapters of this book were first published as Supplements in the *Christian News-Letter*. Before that, they had existed as sections of papers which were written for a small group of friends in the middle years of the war.

The material was edited for the *Christian News-Letter* by Dr J. H. Oldham, to whom acknowledgment is due not only for this, but also and chiefly because without him the original papers would never have been written. It was he who drew together that group of friends who met at intervals, during the years 1938–47, under the name of "the Moot". The group consisted of about a dozen people—not always exactly the same dozen—who differed widely in experience, character, and outlook, but were united in a concern for the recovery of realism in Christian thinking and action. It was not an exclusively Christian group. There were always non-Christians in it, who played an important part by challenging the Christians to see themselves as they really are and their situation as it really is in the modern world. In this connection it would be impossible to exaggerate our debt to the late Karl Mannheim, who told us that we must learn to see ourselves through a sociologist's eyes, and taught us how to begin to do it. Other members of the Moot, however, and above all Dr Oldham himself, had the same sense of a gap between the customary language and thought-habits of Christians and the facts of the present-day world. It was not that we thought Christianity should lower its banner or take to itself the thought-habits of the modern world. On the contrary, we thought that Christians should become more keenly aware of what their Faith is and of what the world is, in order that the real relation between the two may be seen.

To see what the Faith really is—that is the purpose of these chapters. They are an attempt by a Christian to stand away from himself and analyse his own intellectual behaviour. Such self-examination is the proper function of philosophy, and has often been applied to the analysis of scientific thinking. To apply it to Christian thinking is a task less frequently attempted, but is surely an important part of the enterprise which the Moot set before itself—to learn to see what one is really doing as a Christian, and so get rid of false claims and self-deceptions. The other part of the enterprise—to learn to see that world as it is and assess it truly from a Christian point of view—cannot be carried out unless the self-analysis has first been done. It was Dr Oldham's perception of this which led him to inspire the writing of these chapters in the first place, and to arrange them for the *Christian News-Letter*. I wish they were a more adequate response to his challenge.

H. A. HODGES.

I

Christian Thinking

THOSE who really believe in God cannot help thinking and speaking of him. If he has graciously allowed us to know something of himself, we cannot help trying to let others know as much. All real belief is prone to evangelize. This holds good without reference to place or date, it is true everywhere and always. But just as the question of Christian action becomes significant only when it is made concrete and has specific reference to our own time and the present social system, so the question of Christian evangelism, and of the thinking about the Faith which must precede and govern it, needs to be given a similar concrete reference. It is only when it is so treated that it ceases to be an edifying generalization and becomes a question of immediate urgency. *In the present intellectual situation* what is, or should be, Christian thinking and teaching?

What situation in particular do I mean? I mean the common intellectual atmosphere, the prevailing ideas and attitudes, the things which the average man takes for granted and the questions which he is interested in seeing answered. These things have a background, of course, both in the history of thought as such, and in those wider perspectives where ideas and social conditions interact. In both spheres the chief influence has been and is that of science, pure and applied, which has taken for its motto "Knowledge is power", and illustrated it so well in its own way that it has become the standard by which all claims to knowledge and truth are judged. Both in the sphere of theoretical inquiry and in that of technical application it has reached results which flatter the power impulses in man, suggesting that there is no secret which we cannot unveil and no force which we cannot harness. The industrial system, which is the direct outcome of applied science, has had the same effect, causing us to regard the material world as a subject for exploitation, and making competition the normal relation between individuals and groups. The cult of power has affected very deeply the ideals and moral standards of the people, as a score of popular advertisements bear witness.

In a world like this it is inevitable that religion should not be at the hub of things. It survives, and is often able to make some sort of a show of influence, but it is an influence which cannot operate on the levels where the really determinative decisions are made. The Church lives on as an institution, venerable for its antiquity, woven into the habits of the people, and continuing to function by the sheer inertia of tradition. Among its members, and among a large section of the outside public, it maintains by its very existence the habit of certain emotional attitudes and the profession of certain standards which are sometimes revered as embodying an ideal which we recognize but cannot reach, and sometimes jeered at as a dream which cannot come to terms with the facts of life. There is also the social function of the Church as a club, sometimes exploited and used as an advertisement by the Church itself. In short, the Church survives partly by habit and partly because it serves purposes extrinsic to its own essence.

How do we, who profess full adherence to the Christian Faith and make a serious attempt to practise it, appear in the eyes of those who do not? To some we appear inexplicably blind, and they wonder how we can live in the same world as they, with the same resources of knowledge and criticism, and (as they kindly admit) with a respectable degree of intelligence, and yet avoid the conclusions which are so clear to them. We seem to them to be living anachronisms; cf. Trotsky's remarks about the Pope, who is modern enough and enlightened enough to know and use the wireless, but uses it for the hopelessly anachronistic purpose of broadcasting his blessing *urbi et orbi*. They may go further and suspect that our blindness is pathological, like a friend of mine who, on the occasion of my conversion, took a course of reading in Freud in the hope of discovering what was the matter with me. Or again, they may go yet further and regard our blindness as deliberate, as the expression of a hostility to the progress of knowledge and freedom.

And how do we appear to ourselves? We cannot take ourselves for granted so thoroughly as never to make comparisons between ourselves and the non-Christians who surround us. Christian preachers and writers often affect to pity the non-Christian. It is he who is blind, and his blindness may be traced, as he traces ours, to pathological reasons or even to an underlying hostility—in this case a hostility to God and to self-knowledge or discipline. By contrast with him we are the clear-sighted people, the people who are able to weigh evidence impartially, and are free enough from prejudice to see the truth about life and the world. I doubt whether even the man in the pew has really this somewhat complacent conception of himself; and we, who belong to the Christian intelligentsia, do we think of ourselves in this way? Are we sure that our failure to agree with our contemporaries is not sometimes due to a failure to understand them, and that there is not in us a blindness comparable with that which we are taught to discern in them? It is a thought which will not let itself be stifled.

TWO OUTLOOKS IN CONFLICT

How far ought those of us who are not professional theologians to cultivate the knowledge and understanding of our Faith? In every subject there are experts and non-experts, and in this matter, as in every other, the experts are naturally few. A theologian or a spiritual teacher may be no authority on physics, and may rightly leave it to those who are so to settle the subtler questions of quantum theory. In the same way may not the physicist, even if he is also a Christian, leave the details

3

of doctrine for systematic theologians to settle, and depend on a wise and experienced guide in the subtleties of the spiritual life? Clearly he may. But what is the range of the questions which he can rightly leave to experts? Do they include the question how his Christian faith is related to his physics? I myself was once asked whether I did or did not try to find a common ground on which my Christianity and my philosophy could meet. The question was surely absurd. However it may be with a physicist, a philosopher cannot let two sides of his intellectual life stay unco-ordinated. He is bound to take seriously the question of the relation between them.

If the physicist analyses the situation fully he will perhaps have to adopt the same position himself. For his physics is a branch of that scientific activity which has dominated the thought and life of modern times and makes them so different from the thought and life of the age in which Christianity was born. Behind the activity of the individual physicist stands the scientific attitude of mind, with its distinctive distribution of emphases and its distinctive presuppositions—in short, a whole outlook on life and the world. Christianity is also such an outlook. It is no secret to anyone that there is a strain between these two ways of looking at the world. Anyone who is alive to the real issues of life may well find himself driven to come to terms with this tension within himself. Unless he does he is not one man, but two.

The same holds good, in truth, for him and for me and for all of us, at least those of us who are not ministers of religion. For each of us there is a duality of our work in the world and our Christianity; for each of us our work in the world is part and parcel of the modern order of things; for each of us, therefore, the duality of work and religion is more than a duality, it is a tension. And we cannot act responsibly, as unified personalities, unless the tension is in principle overcome. Here is our problem. Our non-Christian friends ask in bewilderment: "How can you do it?" Precisely: how can we do it?

There are two obvious temptations which consist in not facing the tension at all, but running away from it. The one

4

is to let our Christianity go, or at least to force it into the framework of the modern system of ideas at whatever cost to itself. That was the error of the modernists, and I shall say no more here about that. The other temptation is to let the other side of ourselves go, to hark back to an earlier age when the intellectual atmosphere was, or seems to us now to have been, more congenial to Christianity, and to dwell spiritually in that age. This is the way which has been taken by many people concerned in the Catholic revival of the last century: archaism in church architecture and decoration, in vestments and ceremonial, in the content of their theology, in their philosophical background, together with a critique upon the Renaissance and the Reformation and the Industrial Revolution which not merely pointed out their many errors and weaknesses, but wrote them off altogether as a perversity from which we must now recover and start again as before. This is a hopeless line to take in any case, because it is impossible to undo what has been done. But it is also wrong, and amounts to an implicit atheism, or at least to a heresy which denies God's lordship over history.

THE FUNCTION OF PHILOSOPHY

It is to deal with situations like this that philosophy has been called into being. Philosophers are to the intellect what psycho-analysts are to the emotional and appetitive life. They are needed because there are conflicts, not only in people's desires and feelings, but also in their presuppositions and principles, which give rise to incoherences in thought and life. Slight incoherences need not worry anyone, but incoherences in first principles and fundamental attitudes, if neglected, may avenge themselves terribly. A philosopher's business is to look for symptoms of such conflicts, and to work back by epistemological analysis toward their causes. His weapon is the twofold question: What do you mean? and How do you know? which he turns upon every statement made in the field where a conflict is suspected. And people react in three ways. They may ignore him and refuse to examine themselves. Or they may yield to his questioning, and a weakly held conviction may collapse under his assault and leave a blank. (It was for producing this effect that Socrates died.) Or a deeply rooted conviction in a vigorous mind may be purged and strengthened, its meaning clarified and its grounds made visible; and this is what the philosopher hopes will happen, the result he works for.

If we apply this to our present problem it will appear that we need a philosophic inquiry into the real meaning of the contending ways of looking at the world, their fundamental presuppositions and principles, and the grounds on which these rest. But one half of this task is already accomplished for us by the patient labour of modern philosophy. For this is just what modern philosophy is about. It came into play at the time when the new scientific method was struggling to establish itself in a world which had been brought up to think along quite other lines. The scientific workers found themselves asking a new kind of question, answering it by a new method with rather different assumptions from what had been customary, and so revealing a different sort of universe. An issue arose between traditional metaphysics and new science, and the seventeenth and eighteenth centuries were the age in which the issue was fought out. Whatever mistakes may have been made in detail by Kant and his successors, the essentials of their work stand firm. They made clear in outline what the first principles of the modern scientific outlook are, and where their strength lies. The scientific mind sets out to deal with events in time and space. Its ambition is to correlate them within a framework of general laws, allowing of prediction, which shall cover all observable facts with the minimum of assumptions. It is found that the categories of the traditional metaphysics are unnecessary for this purpose, and therefore stand condemned by Ockham's razor; and the final outcome is a view of the world which wavers between idealism and positivism—two philosophies more intimately related than appears on the surface.

The foundations of the modern outlook have thus been subjected to analysis already in the way we have in mind. Our task is thus halved. All that we have to do is to apply the same kind of analysis to our belief in God and Christ. I shall be told that this, too, has already been done, that the question of the possibility of theological knowledge was as much a standing problem in the medieval philosophies as that of the possibility of scientific knowledge is in the modern ones. It was so; but it was the question of the possibility of theological knowledge in a world indelibly tinged with metaphysical ideas and prejudices. The points from which the medievals start in their account of theological thinking include some which have been gravely shaken by what has happened since their time. And therefore their solutions will not stand to-day, at least without a very thorough overhaul. For us, as I said earlier, the problem is that of Christian thinking to-day, and it is a problem to be approached with open minds.

What is urgently needed is an inquiry into the forms or attitudes of imagination and thought which are distinctive of the religious, and specifically of the Christian mind, on the assumption that these will differ from the forms of imagination and thought which underlie other and competing systems of ideas. It is a contribution to logic, in the broadest sense of that term, and it might be called *The Logic of Christian Thinking*. There is plenty of work to be done in this field before the religious consciousness shall have been as well analysed as the scientific consciousness, and only then can the issue between the two be seen for what it is.

We Christians of to-day are on both sides of the cleft. We are modern people, which means not merely that we live in this year and not five centuries ago, but also that we take an active part in the work and life of that society whose mind is dominated by scientific ideas and whose living conditions are determined by industry. But we are also Christians, members of an institution which stays in the organism of present-day society like a foreign body, inheriting a tradition whose relevance to life is less and less obvious, and talking among ourselves a language unintelligible to the non-Christians who surround us. They know that we are Christians, in the sense of knowing that we belong to this institution, and talk this

7

strange language, but they do not know what we mean by it, and for various reasons we are not making them see it. Our Christianity is not something which our non-Christian contemporaries have seen and rejected. They have never seen it. We have failed to make it visible to them in the first place. Or sometimes a few of them get a glimpse of it from afar, but find that they cannot understand what they see. Or they understand, or think they do, but yet fail to be interested. One hears of people saying that they see what we mean, but find it irrelevant or a bore.

Our problem is, therefore, in the first instance that of making Christianity visible again, of making people see it as a really possible way of looking at things. Secondly, we have to try to make it intelligible, so that anyone who sees it as a vision may be able to assure himself that it is not a mirage. The first is a poet's business and the second is a philosopher's. Both are concerned in the third task which faces us, namely to make it appear desirable; to discover and draw out those impulses in humanity which it is meant to satisfy, so that the relevance and the excellence of it may be felt. Are we sure that it is now as visible, intelligible, and obviously desirable even to ourselves as it ought to be?

One may suffer from a division of consciousness and not know it. In that case one is not unaffected by the evil, but its effect is felt as an emotional state, an uneasiness, a restlessness, an inhibition and indecision which makes action ineffective. Is this the condition of the Church to-day? And when in the natural course of things the division threatens to make itself conscious, in order that it may be recognized and healed, we may either face it or shirk it in the interests of self-esteem and comfort. To shirk it means refusing to admit the truth about ourselves, painting a complacent picture of our own state, and ascribing the evil which is the cause of our trouble to someone else. The result of this is continued discontent, sterility, and a growing loss of contact with reality.

If the harder way is taken, and the division of consciousness is not denied but accepted as a fact, we have a course equally uncomfortable, but less sterile. It is a course of patient self-examination in the presence of God, in which first of all our misconceptions will be purged away, and then the truth can be vouchsafed to us. We shall have to ask ourselves over and over again questions of the following kind: What do we mean by "God"? What do we mean by "believing in God"? What is it that we do when we say we "believe"? Why do we do it? Why cannot we help doing it? How do we differ from those who cannot do it? When they ask us by what right we do it, what is our answer? How far do we share their attitude to things called secular? And so on. We must ask these questions and subject every answer to careful examination, so that the merely conventional, or traditional, or re-assuring formulae may be detected and rejected, and the real issue be seen as it is. There is no way to the truth except through this purgation, and the purgation may take long. It may be the destiny of this generation of the Church to enter into a real dark night of the intellect and go through the experience of being forsaken by our false gods before we are shown the face of the true God. But the true God is himself the darkness, and our ignorance, when we face it, is the beginning of knowledge.

2

The Abrahamic Presupposition

THIS chapter and those which follow will deal with certain
aspects of Christianity which seem to me to be central. These
are in themselves not new. How could they be? If it is possible
for new discoveries to be made in Christian truth, I am not the
man to make them. Nor are they exhaustive. Again, I could
not aspire to make them so. But they are the best starting-
point I could find for the purpose announced in my last chapter, to analyse the Christian way of thinking. By this I mean
discovering the reasons by which Christian belief is upheld
and the logical links between its several parts, which are not
always the same as the arguments used in its defence by
apologists writing for the outer public, or for the non-
Christian in themselves.

I do not mean that all or even most Christians reach their
belief by thinking their way to it along the line of argument
here set forth; the argument in parts claims only to formulate
the reasons which operate obscurely in the Christian sub-
consciousness, and which account for the feeling of evidence
with which a belief, whose traditional intellectual supports
have suffered grave damage, still takes possession of many
minds. On what do I rest this contention? On the facts that
(*a*) the more I interrogate my own mind, the more clear it
becomes that these are my own real reasons for believing, in
so far as I have reasons at all; that (*b*) I think I see signs of the
same forces at work in the way other people argue or expound
their faith; and that (*c*) the argument here given seems to
me to be coherent and capable of sustaining the weight of
belief.

Christianity is a more far-reaching system of ideas than non-Christians or indeed many Christians realize, and cannot be expressed, explained, or defended in a few words. By "far-reaching" I mean that it makes a difference to our conception of everything, and not merely of certain things. If someone imbued with the philosophy of scientific naturalism embarks for the first time on the study of psychology, that will alter his conception of the human mind in various details, but it will leave his world-framework untouched. If the same person becomes a Christian, it is precisely the world-framework which will be the first thing to be altered, and changes of detail will follow from this. Even nature is seen differently; not, of course, that Christians have different formulae for the laws of nature, but that they have different ideas of what those laws represent. The same is true of all human activities and values. Thus the adoption of Christianity represents a total change of mind, intellectual as well as moral, and to present its credentials is to show how this change of mind is justified.

To this question there can be no short answer, and none at all until the nature of Christianity, and of the change of mind which it requires, is understood. Exposition and explanation are an absolute prerequisite of defence. My concern in what follows is primarily with explanation, though the two things cannot be kept rigidly apart. To explain a system of ideas, if it is a reasonable system, is to exhibit it as reasonable, which is in itself a recommendation; and besides, I shall be explaining not only what Christians believe, but how the belief arises and how it works itself out and justifies itself in their own minds, so that the explanation will carry an essential element of defence within itself.

It is necessary to begin in this way because an understanding of Christianity cannot be presupposed, even in those who are interested in and friendly to it. In particular they fail to realize how far-reaching it is. They frame their questions and expect to get an answer within their own non-Christian world-framework, thus presupposing that Christianity is not a whole, but a detail. We are expected to start with scientific naturalism or something similar and argue to Christianity as an addition to, or an embellishment of, or a conclusion within this. The task has often been attempted by Christians, and a good deal of traditional apologetic consists in this attempt. I believe that it was once possible to make a show of doing this, but that it was always a circular argument, and that the conditions which made it possible have ceased to prevail. We have now to begin by putting in the foreground the inclusive character of Christianity as a world-framework, and the challenge which it implies to all other such frameworks.

BASIC INTERESTS

The difference between one man's world-framework and another's reflects the difference between their basic interests. Thus it may fairly be said that scientific naturalism is the expression of an interest in knowledge about the spatio-temporal world in that sense in which knowledge is power. Knowledge, or power, or the two linked together, are the main object of the scientific naturalist's aspiration, and this means that the reality in which he is most interested is natural law. From this initial set of interest flow necessarily the methods and presuppositions of the working scientist.

What occupies in Christianity the same central position which the laws of nature hold in scientific naturalism? God; and God may be defined here (the definition is preliminary and must be dogmatic at this early stage) as a being other than ourselves who embodies and exceeds our highest ideal, and with whom we can enter into relations. That this is the central object of interest in Christianity is unnoticed by many, even among Christians; listen to them talking, and see how often their talk circles about morality, or human destiny, or some other object which is not God, and how often God is treated as a counter, of uncertain value, to be played in a dialectical game on such subjects. But the evidence of the most authentic Christian literature and liturgy, with that of the individuals most deeply committed to Christianity in all ages, establishes that the real central object is God, and that everything else which interests the Christian does so because of some relation in which it stands to God.

This determines the task of our inquiry. We must explore the idea of God and its ramifications, discovering what form it takes in the minds of Christians, how it is related to other ideas which offer rival accounts of the nature of ultimate reality, what questions arise when our interest is focused upon it, and how Christians try to answer them.

THE FOUNDATIONS OF CHRISTIAN BELIEF

The idea of God is not one which we construct, as we construct the idea of a horse, from observation of the object itself. We learn of him first by hearsay, for we are born into a world where his name is in constant use; and for many people he remains a matter of hearsay as long as they live. But whence did the idea of God arise in the first instance? It has a history, much of which is known, but its origins are lost in obscurity. To call it innate is merely to shirk the labour of thought. The commonest view is that it arose in some way out of man's attempts to interpret the universe. Such interpretation always works from the familiar to the unfamiliar, and it would be easy to project a magnified human figure as the agent behind mysterious but apparently purposive natural phenomena. Perhaps the root idea may have been something like the Eldest Magician in Kipling's story of *The Crab that Played with the Sea*. But the origin of the idea matters little in comparison with the more developed forms which it has assumed.

The first recorded attempt to establish theism by argument was the work of Anaxagoras, and its basis was astronomy. To the Psalmist, indeed, the heavens declared the glory of God; but he did not argue the case, he looked at the heavens and "saw" there the work of a God in whom he already believed. Anaxagoras did something essentially different. He found that astronomical reasoning contained premises from which the existence of a kind of God naturally followed. Plato and

Aristotle were able to formulate more recondite arguments which resembled Anaxagoras' work in that they started from the facts of nature as interpreted by contemporary thought. The argument from motion began with the fact that things change, interpreted this fact in terms of the categories of act and potency and the principle of the priority of act to potency, and so proved the existence of an unmoved mover. The argument from finitude began with the fact that there are degrees of being, interpreted this fact in terms of the categories of essence and existence and the principle that what exists in varying degrees must also exist in an absolute degree, and so proved the existence of a supreme being in which essence and existence were one. To these was added the more popular argument from design, based especially upon the facts of organic life.

These arguments are logically valid, granted the premises; and the premises constituted, throughout ancient and medieval times, apart from the opposition of the atomists, the agreed presuppositions of natural science and metaphysics. They thus represented a successful attempt to do what the scientist still expects us to do, namely, to argue from his premises to our own conclusion. But the happy change which came over scientific method 300 years ago has had for one of its consequences the disappearance of these categories and principles. They have gone so completely that it is not easy even to explain them to a modern scientific mind. Because of this they have also gradually faded out of philosophy. The new categories and principles which have replaced them are not such as to carry theistic implications, in spite of the gallant attempts of modern philosophers to show that they do. The traditional apologetic is thus left hanging in the air, and the attempts to argue theist conclusions from scientific or metaphysical premises cannot be sustained.

We are thus brought back to an earlier point. Christian thinking does not take its origins from ideas or principles which belong to any world-framework other than its own. What, then, are the first principles, other than those of science and peculiar to itself, from which it begins?

The study of scientific method by logicians in the last 300 years has led to certain conclusions which are generally accepted. It is recognized that the secret of progress in natural science lies in a combination of mathematics with observation and experiment, and that the aim of the method so constituted is to discover regularities in the sequence of events. It is recognized also that in doing this the scientist consciously or unconsciously presupposes something. He presupposes that regularities of the kind he is seeking are really there to be found, and that they are such as can be expressed mathematically. In spheres of inquiry where mathematics are less applicable, as in the human studies, the inquiry is still governed by the search for regularities. Even in history, which is often said to be, and in some sense is, a study of the concrete individual, what makes the difference between mere chronicling and genuine historical study is the presence in the latter of a consciousness of general principles underlying the course of events. In all these spheres the presupposition of regularity is made.

It is this presupposition which makes the whole inquiry possible. The question, what is the law of this phenomenon, does not arise unless we assume or take for granted that there is a law. If we do presuppose this, the question arises progressively over the whole field of experience, and scientific methods spring into existence as the means of answering it. This is what gives the presupposition its peculiar logical position. It is not open to question, and yet this is not because we know it to be true. It cannot be established either *a priori*, since it is not self-evident, or *a posteriori*, by the evidence of facts, since it is this presupposition itself which gives facts their force as evidence. For the same reason, of course, there can be no evidence against it. It stands above the region in which evidence is weighed and conclusions are drawn; but when it is presupposed, it turns every fact into evidence of other facts, and leads to an indefinite widening and co-ordinating of experience. For this reason, and because the results of a successful search for law in experience are so important to us, we *refuse* to question the presupposition which makes this search possible, and which is prejustified by the fact that we cannot begin the inquiry without it, and postjustified by the success of the inquiry when made.

The *refusal* is not an intellective act, an apprehension of truth, but what I should like to call a *basic acceptance*. It is the choosing to explore a certain form of thought and experience, with a readiness to accept whatever we shall find there and submit to its influence upon our outlook, character, and destinies. This fact is what some modern apologists have tried to express by saying that at the basis of every branch of experience, even science, lies an act of "faith". This word, however, carries so many associations which are not relevant at this point, that I think it better not to use it, and to speak instead of a *basic acceptance*.

As a presupposition is not something known, so also it is not a theory or a hypothesis. Theories or hypotheses are ways of applying our presupposition to the available facts. A theory unites a group of diverse facts by exhibiting in them a single principle of form, and claims our assent so long as it does this. It is justified in so far as further inquiry verifies it, but it remains always open to modification in the light of fresh facts. But a presupposition is unaffected by the discovering of fresh facts. It is what makes both the theory and its modification by fresh facts possible.

THE ABRAHAMIC PRESUPPOSITION

Now, I shall contend that Christian thinking proceeds on a presupposition of its own, which I shall call *the Abrahamic Presupposition*, or *Abrahamic Theism*. For the New Testament insists over and over again that Abraham is the model for Jew and Christian alike, and that the true Christian is the spiritual child of Abraham, i.e. one whose relation to God is the same as Abraham's was. And here it does not matter whether the life story of Abraham as set forth in Genesis and interpreted in Romans and Hebrews is literal history or not. The point is that it gives us the standard by which our attitude to life is to be regulated, if it is to be a Christian attitude.

Abraham in the story is a man who has committed himself unconditionally into the hands of God; a man who does what God asks of him without hesitation, however paradoxical or self-contradictory it may seem, and who accepts God's promises, however mysterious and incredible they may appear. It is by virtue of this unconditional self-commitment to God that he has won the title of the Friend of God. But such an attitude evidently presupposes a great deal. It presupposes not merely the existence of God, about which the philosophers have debated so lengthily, but that God is of a certain character. It presupposes that God has complete control of the world and the course of events in it; that he exercises this control in a way which is purposeful; that human beings have a place in his designs; and that he communicates with them in ways which they can legitimately understand as commands and promises, and by which their lives can be guided. This is the presupposition of Jewish and Christian thinking, which I call Abrahamic theism. To work it out in detail, showing how it applies in actual life and thought, is the business of theology.

The Abrahamic presupposition differs in obvious ways from the scientific presupposition, but it has the same logical properties and status. It is not a self-evident truth, nor a piece of knowledge gathered from experience, but a presupposition made as a result of a basic acceptance. It is prejustified because it enables us to open up a field of experience which cannot be opened up without it, and discoveries in which, if made, would have a close bearing on human interests. It gives facts a new significance, and raises questions and gives rise to theories of a distinctive kind. Its postjustification lies in the fact that theories do arise in this field which cover the known facts, point the way for further inquiries and fresh discoveries, and enable us to act in ways which are important and beneficial.

It is the task of our logic of Christian thinking to explain this in detail.

3
The Metaphysical Presupposition

PHILOSOPHY AND THE GOD OF ABRAHAM

MY last chapter ended by formulating the "Abrahamic presupposition" on which Christian thinking is based. This presupposition in its proper form plays no part in the history of philosophy, and only a limited part in the history of religion itself. It is in Judaism, Christianity, Islam, and Mazdeism that it shows itself most effectively. In the religions of the Far East, and in the philosophies alike of east and west, another principle is seen at work, which may be described as the Abrahamic presupposition *depersonalized*. It retains the idea of purpose at work in nature and history, and it agrees that man can in some degree come to know the cosmic purpose and find his happiness in acting concordantly with it; but it leaves out the element of personal confrontation between God and individual human beings, and explicit communication from God to them, which is contained in Abrahamic theism.

THE METAPHYSICAL PRESUPPOSITION

The principle, so depersonalized, might be formulated thus: *that the universe is governed by a purpose to whose nature our own highest intellectual and moral aspirations provide a clue.* This principle I call *the metaphysical presupposition*.

This presupposition is what Hegel meant by saying that the real is the "rational" and the "rational" is the real. It has often been used since his time as the basis of an argument for the existence of God on the ground that the world must be assumed to be "rational", and that a world without God is "meaningless" or does not ultimately "make sense". But the word "rational" is ambiguous. It may mean "purposive", and imply all that the metaphysical presupposition asserts; or it may merely mean "knowable", which implies not the metaphysical presupposition, but the scientific. And there is an equivocation in a certain kind of Christian apologetics which begins with the proposition that the world is "rational" in the scientific sense, and slides unconsciously into assuming that it is also "rational" in the sense of the metaphysical presupposition. The second does not follow from the first, and it was one of Kant's services to philosophy to point this out. If we are going to assume the metaphysical presupposition, we had better be explicit about it, and not try to extract it from the principles of science.

The two presuppositions were clearly distinguished by Plato when he wrote the *Phaedo*. He paints a picture of Socrates becoming dissatisfied with a philosophy which is merely physics, and calling for an account of the universe which shall be based on "the binding force of good". Here is the birth of Platonism and of the whole classical tradition in European philosophy. But as that tradition developed, even in the hands of its founders, Plato and Aristotle, the two principles originally distinguished were run together into one. The metaphysical presupposition was imported into the foundations of science itself, and we were told that all existence and all process or movement is governed by an inherent purposiveness. If this were so, then the principles of science would contain elements on which an argument for the existence of God could be based, and the classical European tradition contends that this is the case. But I believe that the principles thus imputed to science were alien principles foisted upon it from outside, that they were derived from the metaphysical presupposition, and that their acceptance was one of the causes of the sterility of science for 2,000 years. In modern times they have been detected and dismissed, and the classical equivocation disappears with them. If anyone is going to argue from the metaphysical presupposition to-day, he must do so with full consciousness of what he is doing.

Now, I believe that the typical Christian in his own thinking does not make the metaphysical presupposition. He makes the Abrahamic presupposition which I described in my last chapter. The metaphysical presupposition is a dim shadow of that in the minds of people who are not bold enough to make the full Christian presupposition all in one jump. But I believe that if you start with the metaphysical presupposition, as so many do, and seek the most effective way of applying it to the facts of experience, the most effective way will be found in fact to be Abrahamic theism. And thus those who do not take to it at first may be led to it indirectly. How would the argument run?

When the metaphysical presupposition is at work in the mind, conditioning our interpretation of the facts of experience, it may give rise to any one of a number of theories: animism, polytheism, monotheism, panpsychism, pantheism, philosophical idealism. These theories are not all equally deserving of consideration. There is in human thinking a persistent tendency to seek simplicity and to reduce the welter of facts in the world to a unity. By virtue of this tendency the many gods or spirits of primitive belief tend to disappear, or at least to be brought under a single governing power. The pluralistic theories therefore need not detain us, and I shall group all remaining theories under the two heads of pantheism and theism; pantheism for this purpose is to include idealist philosophies of the classic post-Kantian type. These two theories differ only in the point where they place the purpose which is held to govern nature. Pantheism places it in nature itself, which is taken to be a consciously or unconsciously purposive whole; theism places it in a conscious being distinct from nature.

By what methods can we decide between these rival views? (i) Not by direct observation. The God of theism is not open to observation, and while the God of pantheism is so, he does not look as the theory says he is. (ii) Not indirectly by the test of consequences, as scientific hypotheses are established, for (at the present stage in the argument) there are no consequences in the field of observable facts which would follow from one of the rival theories and not from the other. (iii) There is then no test left to us but the formal one which is used in philosophical speculation, of showing that a theory, while coherent and reasonable in itself, colligates all the known facts in the manner laid down by the governing presupposition. This test appears weak at first sight, especially in view of the age-long confusion in speculative philosophy. But I think it could be shown that this confusion is due to the philosophers not having been in earnest with the metaphysical presupposition, some of them not having held it at all, and others having tried to blend it with the scientific presupposition as I have already explained. I think also that, if we are really in earnest with it, we shall find that only theism can stand the test, and even theism can do so only if it takes a particular form.

THE DIFFICULTIES OF PANTHEISM

On the ground of coherence and reasonableness, pantheism attracts by its air of simplicity, especially in a world which has learned from science the value of economy in explanation. Where theism needs two entities, God and nature, pantheism makes do with one. To this logical point may be added the aesthetic appeal of a doctrine of one all-embracing Whole, which can be felt at work in some modern philosophers. On further consideration, however, difficulties begin to arise. The world as we see it or as science reveals it is not the divine Whole which pantheism says it is, and so we are driven to say that the divine unity is only one aspect of the world—the deepest and truest aspect, of course—which is hidden from common sense and science, but revealed to poets, worshippers, and philosophers. Yet at the same time the world of common sense and science is not illusory; it, too, has to be an aspect of the real. So we must try to hold together two aspects of reality which continually threaten to fuse or to come apart. The empirical universe is always with us, and it is hard to remember that this is not the "Nature" which we are to regard as God. It is equally hard to see what that something more can be, which constitutes the aspect of divine wholeness in it. How a universe which to empirical investigation appears purposeless can also be purposive is especially hard to see. It is clear how a machine, in itself without purpose, can express the purposes of its maker and user; but pantheism asks us, as it were, to put purposivity into the machine itself. Apart from the difficulty of seeing how what is mechanical is at the same time inherently purposive, there is difficulty in conceiving the kind of purposivity to be attributed to it. If it is to be unconscious, there are metaphysical problems in this. If conscious, what is the centre or centres of such consciousness? It can happen that theism appears as a relief from perplexities like these.

Nor is this all. Even if we pass over the difficulty of understanding how the pantheist's universe can have a purpose at all, there is still a difficulty in understanding what its purpose can be. In the present state of knowledge, with the story of the evolution of life on this planet now well known, most people will naturally look there for a clue. But what do we find there? Of all the various qualities and capacities which evolution has thrown up in living things and especially in man, which are to be regarded as the really important ones, for whose sake the whole process has been gone through? What qualities contribute most to survival and further development? A combination of strength and cunning? So Nietzsche would say, and a strong body of opinion with him. Or social co-operation? So says another strong body of opinion, which sees the goal of evolution in a peaceful human society embracing the whole of mankind. But even then we must ask what kind of society it is to be. Is it the beehive type, with a closely co-ordinated system of functions and a strict regimentation of its members, where the system is all and the people are made to serve it? Or is it a society where the system serves the indi-

22

viduals, and everything is done to encourage diversity? Which of the types of relationship that can subsist between men is the really central and significant one? Is it the political relation? Or is it the intimate relations which hold between individuals in small groups of friends? Intellectual and spiritual growth seems to be closely bound up with this latter kind of relationship. Is this side of human nature the central fact and value of the whole, or is it a by-product of social and political processes, which must wait upon their convenience? We are not agreed among ourselves about this. But those who find the highest of values in the intellectual and spiritual life, and in the most intimate relationships between people, will also find that these values are precarious and fragile. If the highest aspirations of man are a clue to the cosmic purpose, as the metaphysical presupposition asserts, should this be so? And wherever in the sphere of life we find the highest value, we have to face the apparent inevitability of the final destruction of all life by the cooling of the sun.

THE DIFFICULTIES OF THEISM

Theism, in turn, raises problems of its own, of which the chief is to make intelligible the relation between God and the world. I do not mean merely the question of the nature and mode of operation of the divine causality. I mean also the question why God should produce a universe at all. The theory that it emanates from him by a natural necessity, without his either willing it or being able to help it, cannot be established, because there is no means of showing such a natural necessity. But if not this, the production of the world must be a deliberate act on God's part, and therefore purposive. And if so, what can the purpose be? Merely to exercise power and cunning in giving existence to a world which he then leaves to itself? Even a man can do better than that; he finds the core of his life in his relations with other human beings and with animals, and even treats his material possessions and the works of his hands with a playful pretence of finding in them a personal response. (Personification of ships, etc.) Since God's world contains beings who can at least conceive the possibility of entering into reciprocal relations with him, it is natural to conclude that he made it so on purpose, and controls its history with the overriding aim of entering into relations with mankind (and with any other such beings as may happen to exist: we do not actually know of any others). We are led to think of him as so fashioning the world that it becomes a means of communication between him and us, a vehicle by which he teaches and guides us. His purpose must include what is best in ours, but at the highest level of integration, and it is to this that he must be taking us.

No conception of God is really coherent and reasonable unless it goes as far as this. But if it does go so far it promises to deal with the question of human values more effectively than pantheism could. It centres everything on a relationship which is of the most intimate and personal kind, and which touches each man not by virtue of his social place and function, but of what is most individual and distinctive in him. And it at least gives us a chance of dealing with the problem of death: for a God who is distinct from the world may enter into relations with us which lead beyond the present order of space and time. But of this more in detail in our next chapter.

PERSONAL RELATIONS AT THE HEART OF THINGS

It should be noted that in this last lap the argument has by-passed Anaxagoras and all the Greek tradition of philosophical theism, with its distant and unconcerned God, and has come to a position more akin to that which is associated by tradition with the names of Abraham the Friend of God, and Moses with whom he spoke face to face.

This is of the highest importance; for it means that the only way of applying the metaphysical presupposition satisfactorily to the facts is by a theory which puts personal relationships at the heart of things. We are in a recognizably Judaeo-Christian atmosphere, for it is these two religions above all which have used personality and personal relations as the key to reality, and set up the archetypes of the family,

24

father, children, brethren, etc., in heaven and on earth. We have got away from all purely political hierarchies like Olympus, all impersonal Absolutes and all unconcerned Supreme Intelligences. And what is true in theology must be true also in ethics. We are out of the ambit of moral theories based on self-contained perfection or happiness, though what is true in such theories can be put inside ours; it is for the sake of my brethren in heaven and on earth that I ought to cultivate the virtues which Aristotle analyses so well. We have come beyond the standpoint of all Greek philosophy, though the argument which has brought us here has been throughout a philosophical one.

"God of Abraham, God of Isaac, God of Jacob, not of the philosophers and the learned." These words have been much advertised ever since they were written, but the correct conclusion has not been drawn from them. They have been used as a jibe at the expense of philosophy, and as such they have been a godsend to theologians and pietists who wished to safeguard their thoughts from rational criticism. But this use of Pascal's words rests on the assumption that the gap which he signalizes between Christian theology and philosophy is due to something inherent in the nature of philosophy, whereas in fact it is due to the bad management of the philosophers down to and since Pascal's time. The philosophy of the medieval period learned much from Christianity, but not enough. It brought its conclusions into accord with Christian doctrine, and while taking over the fundamental concepts of Greek ontology it gave them a richer and truer meaning by reading the philosophy of being in the light of the word that was spoken from the burning bush. And yet it did not fully understand this word. I AM is not the whole meaning of EHYEH, though it is certainly contained in it. And the concept of being, so transfigured in the light of that word, ceases surely to be a concept of natural reason. The relation between scientific and religious thinking, and between human religion and the light of revelation, is more complex and subtle than medieval philosophy was able to grasp. On the other hand, the Reformation protest was over-violent and essentially misdirected.

The result should have been not a campaign against philosophy in the interests of "faith", but a deeper analysis of the Christian way of thinking itself, and a re-examination of the great questions in the light of this. It might then have been found that there is built into the foundations of Christianity a philosophy which is deeper and truer, on those points which it touches, than the speculations of the Greeks and their later disciples, and that Philo and his friends were not wholly wrong in saying that Moses had already reached a height in philosophy to which even Plato did not fully rise.

4

The Problem of Evil

THOSE who undertake to interpret experience on the lines indicated in the preceding chapter, in which we considered the problem of Theism, are faced at the outset by the great and complex problem of evil. Christianity has its own way of dealing with this, and we must now see what this way is.

THE CASE AGAINST GOD

The facts upon which the case against God is based are too well known to need detailed elaboration. Man lives in a world which moves by impersonal laws and is indifferent to the fortunes of life within it. Accident and disease bring pain, frustration, and death; calamity falls upon individuals and species, races and civilizations. In the realm of life itself there are beasts of prey and predatory instincts in others, and in mankind there is even worse, in the shape of moral evil. Neither the evils which befall men from the forces of nature nor those inflicted by other men are distributed according to desert. In particular, it happens that what is morally best in us may contribute to our material downfall; and situations arise in which every course of action open to us is somehow unjust. This seems to make nonsense of moral standards altogether. Finally, the whole race of man lives under sentence of death at the hand of cosmic forces, through the law of entropy if not through anything else, and this makes the whole episode of life seem meaningless. This, in brief, is the indictment.

From this it is commonly inferred that God is lacking in either power or goodness. Most commonly it is his goodness which is denied. He has no care, it is said, for individuals, for communities, for moral principles, even for life itself. A shadow is cast over all optimism about the future of humanity, bewilderment and despair tend to set in. Personal religion becomes impossible, because God seems both inaccessible and undesirable. From the doctrine of an indifferent God we slide further into pantheism or atheism.

Christianity resists these conclusions, of course, and it has several ways of dealing with them. But these ways are not all of equal value, nor all equally native to the Christian mode of thought. My present purpose, therefore, is to sift them from this point of view, so as to see what in them is distinctly Christian.

THE VIEW THAT EVIL IS UNREAL

The doctrine that evil is not a reality, but a kind of nothingness, though of pagan origin, has been adopted by Christian thinkers and has brought light and comfort to many. It is especially bound up with the Christian mystical tradition. It is not a religious doctrine, but a metaphysical one, and when properly understood it is not as absurd or as frivolous as it may seem at first sight. But, however sensible it may be, it is no real answer to the question in hand. For, let evil be ever so much a nothing, it remains a problem why God allows such a nothing to come in where we should expect something. To tell us what evil is to not to tell us that it does not exist, or that it is not evil.

IS GOD THE AUTHOR OF EVIL?

Much Christian teaching of all periods tries to save God's credit by limiting his responsibility, lifting at least the weight of moral evil off his shoulders. The possibility of moral perversion, which has become an actuality in our universe, is, they say, part of the price God and ourselves have to pay for

28

human freedom and responsibility. God has deliberately limited his control over the actions of men, and in consequence he permits things to happen for which we alone, and not he, must bear the blame.

No doubt there is a sense in which it is blasphemy to say that God is the author of evil; yet it is also true that evil could not come into existence unless he granted it existence. And the distinction between God's doing a thing and his allowing it to happen will not avail for the purpose desired. For anyone who could prevent a thing from happening but does not do so must bear some responsibility for it when it happens; and if God freely brings into being a universe which he knows to contain the possibility of evil, he cannot disown a real responsibility for the evil when it materializes. There is no way out along this path. And, indeed, this theological explanation about the price of human responsibility and freedom is not the only word that Christianity speaks on this question. Some passages in the Bible and some systems of theology take quite a different line. They ask us what right the clay has to give back answers to the potter, which means in prose that we are subordinated or even sacrificed, and justly so, to purposes greater than ourselves.

This view has a vertiginous attraction for some. It appeals to our capacity for self-abnegation, and also perhaps to a strain of masochism in us. But it needs careful handling. The whole to which we are subordinated or sacrificed must be of a higher order than ourselves, and the total system of nature, at any rate, is not so; which fact defeats the attempt to use the principle of the higher whole in terms of a pantheist Absolute. Such a higher whole can be conceived only in one of two ways. It may consist of beings higher in the scale of value than we; but such do not seem in fact to exist in any form that could profit by our sufferings. Or it may consist of ourselves in a higher stage of being than we now enjoy, but one which can only be reached through our present struggles. This latter view also satisfies what seems to be a further requirement of justice, that we, as intelligent beings capable of intercourse with God, should not be used even for a higher end without being given a real chance to know it and accept it; for it implies a hereafter in which what is now obscure becomes plain.

THE "PETER WIMSEY" TYPE OF ARGUMENT

This is the Christian mode of argument, according to the model laid down by Christ himself and reported in Mark 12.26–7. Abraham, Isaac, and Jacob are dead; but God, who is the God of the living, declares himself their God; therefore, though dead, they yet live. God, that is to say, never lets go one with whom he has established a personal relationship; so that if he has so fashioned the world as to make it a vehicle for communication with all of us, his purpose must contain a future for all of us.

The argument is like that of a familiar type of detective-story plot, of which Miss Sayer's *Strong Poison* is a good example. We begin with Harriet Vane in the dock and a strong case against her. The police, having no prepossessions in her favour, argue thus: all the known facts are against her, therefore she is guilty. Lord Peter Wimsey, who has a pre-possession in her favour, argues thus: all the known facts are against her; but she is not guilty; therefore the known facts are not all the facts. And then he considers what the other facts must be, and seeks them out and finds them. So we find God arraigned on the strength of the facts of evil, and the world, not having any antecedent interest in God, argues thus: the facts are strongly against him, therefore he is guilty, if he exists at all. We, who have the Abrahamic presupposition, argue thus: the known facts are strongly against him; but he is not guilty; therefore the known facts are not all the facts. And we can infer in a general way what the missing facts must be.

This way of thinking, where we take empirical facts, confront them with our presupposition, and so infer other facts, is very characteristic of the Christian and Jewish mind. Thus human beings die; but human beings are brought into per-sonal relation with God, and so acquire an absolute value;

therefore death is not the end of existence. Or again: the universe, being God's universe, supports and fulfils all that is best in our purposes; but material goods are notoriously transient; therefore material goods are not the main purpose of life, even here and now. Or again: human life is beset by injustice and failure, no society and no culture is free from grave evils; therefore society and culture as we know them now are not the final achievement of mankind. Or again: the physical world as we now see it appears to be doomed to ultimate breakdown through the law of entropy; therefore this world is not the climax of creation.

In the Bible itself we find many similar cases of inference looking towards the future. There is an interesting one imputed to Abraham, which runs thus: Isaac is the child of promise; but he is to die as a sacrificial victim; therefore in some way he will rise from the dead (Heb. 11.17–19). This is from a Christian writer reading back his own ideas into an Old Testament story. But the Old Testament itself argues on the same principle. For instance, God has made covenant with Israel and will not go back from his word; but Israel as a whole is not keeping the terms of the covenant; therefore (a) Israel as a whole must be chastized, but (b) a Remnant shall always carry on the life of the nation. In the Gospels we meet the argument: Jesus is the destined Victor over all evil; but it is plain that he is going to be put to death; therefore he will in some way triumph in and after his death. Later in the New Testament we find the old argument reapplied: the Church is in danger of destruction by her own corruption and by the powers of this world; but the Church is the Body of Christ and the vehicle of God's purpose for mankind; therefore the Harlot and the Beast will be destroyed and the Bride enthroned. All apocalyptic and all eschatology arise in this way, from the confrontation of present fact with a metaphysical or religious presupposition, and the consequent inference to a better future.

The style of argument here described has, up to a point, the same logical form as the arguments of science. The scientist does not find natural law staring him in the face whenever he looks at the world. Quite the contrary. He finds apparent chaos and contingency. But he takes to himself the scientific presupposition, that everything is a case of a law, and fills in the gaps of his observations with inferred causes and inferred effects, just as Christianity comes to the world armed with the Abrahamic or at least the metaphysical presupposition, and simplifies the given facts of experience by adding others to complete the pattern. The difference is that, so far as our exposition has got, Christianity has not yet been shown to have any means of verifying its inferences, while the strength of science lies, of course, in the fact that it can do so. This is not to say that Christian beliefs are not, in their own way, brought to the test of empirical fact and sometimes transformed under its influence. How this comes about will appear later, in this and the following chapter.

Meanwhile, we must guard against taking the Peter Wimsey argument in a too facile way, as is often done both by ill-instructed Christians and by their opponents. The mistake lies in a misinterpretation of the Abrahamic presupposition. Inherent in that presupposition is the confident belief that, since man is called into intimate personal relations with God, and derives from this fact an unconditional value, man cannot fail ultimately to realize all that is worth while in him. The mistake lies in thinking that this guarantees the survival in perpetuity of human beings as they now are, and the final satisfaction of their present hopes and aspirations. In short, it takes man as we find him now, and puts him and his values in the centre of the picture. The belief that Christianity invents its God and the rest of its supernatural apparatus for the sake of making people feel comfortable, of assuring them of security in their world and/or a continuance of their existing selves in another world, is very widespread. It is a just appraisement of the debased Christianity here described, but it cannot survive the analysis of how the mature Christian mind really works. For Abrahamic living involves a readiness to follow God's lead and to commit oneself to his guidance, in the knowledge that he will take us to an unknown land and change us pretty radically in the process. When we respond to his invitation

32

we do so knowing that we are saying good-bye to our present selves, and embarking on a course of self-transcendence no less than of self-preservation or self-development. It is time now to see what this involves more in detail.

ALL EVENTS ARE FROM GOD

God, we saw, must be conceived as governing nature and the course of events in time. In that case all events proceed from him and all situations are his sending. This does not deny the reality of natural causes. But natural causes cannot operate except as they derive power and opportunity to do so from the First Cause; so that no amount of insistence on the inherent powers of the creature can alter the truth of our contention, that in the long run all events proceed from God.

Moreover, we saw that God must be held to direct the course of events in such a way as to guide and instruct us. History is a channel of communication between him and ourselves. This differentiates Christianity at once from the religion of moral virtue which is so often substituted for it in popular belief. For the religion of moral virtue puts the point of contact between God and us in moral precepts, which are given to us by God through reason or revelation in a generalized form, and which we have only to apply to circumstances as they arise. The circumstances in themselves contribute nothing to the moral life; all that is moral (or religious) on this view lies in the general principles. And if, as is theoretically possible, we have studied these principles well enough to get a full understanding of what they say, they are open to no further adjustment, and there is nothing more for history to teach us. Such is the standpoint of Greek ethics. But Christianity makes God the Giver not only of precepts, but also of the circumstances in which we have to act, and the living contact between him and ourselves comes in the course of events, in the moment of action itself. For there a concrete relationship is established with things and people which calls for constant new efforts of understanding and decision, and so yields constantly new insight into the meaning of the principles with which we started.

EVERY SITUATION A GOD-GIVEN OPPORTUNITY

The world's wisdom knows that every situation can be an opportunity. To the Christian, it is a God-given opportunity. It brings about a fresh relationship not only with things and people, as we have just said, but in and through them with God also. It is a confrontation and a challenge. Every power and every possession that is ours is God's gift, and therefore a responsibility. On the other hand, every duty is also his sending, and therefore a gift. For in our dealing with God there is no difference between gifts and demands; everything that comes to us from him is both at once. Every situation is a communication from God, bearing a threefold word. It is a word of command. It is a word of judgement, and the verdict depends on how we have taken the command. It is a word of promise, in that God gives us his commands not merely for his own good pleasure, but for the sake of making out of us something which we are not now and cannot yet conceive.

A life lived on these principles is new from moment to moment. The stability of achieved knowledge and perfected character, the aim of the pagan sage, cannot enter into it. The good pagan stands foursquare against all assaults of fate. The Christian walks with God, moving forward to a goal which only his Guide can clearly see. He is a pilgrim and a sojourner in the world. His life is exploration and novelty, but exploration under guidance, and novelty not created by him but given to him.

This peregrinal element in the Christian life is what is sometimes called its "experimental" character. It plays the part, we are told, in relation to the Christian faith, which experiment to plays in relation to a scientific hypothesis. And no doubt to some extent, and for some people, this is true. We may start with the metaphysical presupposition, and after consideration we may be brought by its inherent logic to a point at which we must make the venture of putting ourselves into God's hands. If we then do so, we find that the promised guidance does appear, that we are not left kicking our heels, or led round in circles, or carried off into a bog, but carried onward in a course which has direction and meaning, though we could not have plotted it for ourselves. The Christian assumption does verify itself in this way, though it is an experiment which only a lifetime can fully work out, and in that respect quite unlike the slick laboratory technique with which we are invited to compare it.

Life lived on this basis gives a certain satisfaction indeed, but it is a little one-sided to speak without qualification of its giving "comfort". It roots up too many fixed habits of mind for that to be possible. The man who lives thus is not making use of God, but being used by God, and remade all the time as he is used. Certainly, as we have said, the word is not only of command, nor only of judgement, but also of promise; but the promise is of gifts beyond our present conceiving, which are to be given to a man re-created. To the existing self it is the labour of a gradual death.

FAITH, HOPE AND LOVE

At this point we can trace the rise of the famous triad of Christian virtues: faith, hope, and love. *Faith* in this context must be understood in the sense which the word bears in St Paul and the writer to the Hebrews, both of whom use (among others) the figure of Abraham to illustrate it. The key to the career of Abraham is his readiness to do without question whatever God invites him to do and to believe the promises which come with the command, though with a minimum of explanation. With this readiness to take God's commands seriously is necessarily bound up the serious acceptance of God's promises for the future, i.e. faith implies *hope*. And both are characteristic of the attitude towards God which is Jewish first, and then Christian, in contradistinction to the Greek view of life. Greek wisdom does not know faith at all. It knows only belief or opinion, which is contrasted discreditably with knowledge; for knowledge is certain, safe, stable, while opinion is shifting, unreliable, misleading. And Greek wisdom knows hope only as the deceiver, to which the sage must learn to shut his ears. A general atmosphere of frustration broods over the Greco-Roman world, and this is not unconnected with the abstractness of pagan philosophy, which finds in God an indifferent Source of Being, and tries to govern life on general moral principles, regarding this world as a prison and action as a sign of impotence. All this comes about because, in Hellenism, God is not effectively Lord of the world, not the Master of history and the Guide and Teacher of man. We see again, more clearly, how truly Moses reached a wisdom far beyond that of the pagans; for the Hebrew God is the Living God from the start and the Friend of man. In face of such a God, faith and hope are a duty.

In such intercourse arises also that generous self-devotion which is Christian love (*agape*). This also is characteristic of Christianity. Whether it is true, as some say, that the pagan world knew nothing of love in this sense at all, may well be doubted; but it is true that that world, in so far as it had a really personal religion at all, found its kernel chiefly in a movement of desire from man to God, the famous *eros*. This has also a place in Christianity, whatever some may say; but it is there to bring us to God, and when it has done that, the confrontation with God kindles the *agape* which dominates and disciplines *eros*.

In the theme of this present section we have, for the first time in the course of this argument, reached a point of contact with the non-Christian thought of our age. The Marxist conception of dialectic is complex and has complex origins; but when Marxists say that action ought to be guided by dialectical thinking, they mean *inter alia* that we must not go by general principles, but by an understanding of the present and ever-changing situation in its wholeness. It is partly for not doing this that they attack "idealism", with which they

36

class all religion. In dialectic so conceived are we not to see a recognition of that day-to-day character of man's life in this world, which Christianity also in fact recognizes? Are we to say that the Marxist is consciously repudiating the false god of the Greeks and unconsciously recognizing the true God who is the Lord of history?

5

The Knowledge of God

In our second chapter we defined God provisionally as a
being, other than ourselves, who embodies and exceeds our
highest ideal, and with whom we can enter into relations.
In the last chapter we examined the meaning of the last clause
of this definition, and now it is time to look into the penul-
timate clause.

GOD AS THE EMBODIMENT OF OUR HIGHEST IDEAL

That this is also an essential part of the conception of God
was plain, among others, to Anselm, who takes it, be it
noted, as a thing generally agreed and needing no argument
that God is to be understood as "that than which a greater
cannot be conceived". The author of the *Proslogion* was not
playing metaphysical games with abstract concepts borrowed
from the philosophy of his time; he was interrogating his own
mind at the moment when he prayed, and finding that it was
to God as the greatest thinkable that he prayed. And finding
this in his own mind as the salient point of its devotion, he
justly concluded that it was the heart of other people's devotion too. Of course, his conception of God had more content
than this, which he spent much of his meditation in explicat-
ing. But it seems that the original formula of "the greatest
thinkable" is what is common to all who worship at all, while
the other details are what vary according to place and time.
Even in the crudest religions, so far as one can see, the gods
are the embodiment of what we should most like to have in
ourselves: power and life.

As ideals grow in depth and complexity with the growth of civilization it seems that each of them in turn becomes attached to the gods and enrolled as a divine attribute. So in course of time the gods become intellectualized and moralized. Still the main character of them remains, they are for civilized men the archetypes of those qualities which they most esteem. The Greek pantheon especially represents this stage, and Greek philosophy takes us on to the next, where all the gods are rolled into one, and he is the synthesis of all archetypes. So, too, of course, is the God of Hebrew monotheism, and the Hebrews took his moral character more seriously than the Greeks, as is natural, since they, rather than the Greeks, entered into personal relations with him.

But thought goes further even than this. In addition to blending all the archetypes as attributes of God, we can ask whether they may not all have a common character, an essential nature of which they are all manifestations. If so, this, of course, would be the essential nature of God, the unity behind the plurality of his attributes. The Greeks and their later pupils found this common character in *being*, so that God was *being* in the fullest sense of the word, or "pure act". Religious thought not biassed by Greek metaphysics seems to prefer the view that all the archetypes are qualities or manifestations of *life*, and God is therefore fullness of life. That is how Bowman exhibits him in his *Studies in the Philosophy of Religion*.[1] God so conceived is no longer merely the synthesis, but the Archetype of archetypes.

GOD AS CREATOR, RULER, AND FRIEND

The control over nature which we have ascribed to God takes its place as one of the archetypes which meet in him, since it is after all a thing which we attempt and in a measure achieve for ourselves. Man does not make the physical world and cannot alter its laws; but he can so far control certain factors within it as to set up a little world of his own, a world of tools, and comforts, and works of art and science, which

[1] Macmillan & Co, 1938.

stand out to some extent as a world within the world, different from and sometimes at odds with the larger whole. The more man's own world develops on its own lines, the more it becomes liable to disturbance by the forces of crude nature outside; and so there grows up the idea of the inscrutable and ineluctable power of fate. But fate is never the whole truth about the world in its relation to us; for the gods are believed to make and maintain the natural order as we make and maintain our own social order, which means that behind the apparent opposition man and the gods are really akin and are doing the same sort of thing. On this basis the gods can be and are appealed to as the reconcilers of man and nature, the rulers of both and givers of harmony and life. The Old Testament goes further. It makes God the Creator and Designer of history, i.e. of situations and opportunities which call out the best in us and make possible a life of friendship with him.

The relationship so established between God and man is closer and more intimate than any which man can have with his fellows. It alone has no limitations, since there is nothing on either side to conceal, and no possibility on man's side of concealing anything. No moment of life is outside this relationship. God "has beset us behind and before, and laid his hand upon us". This is intimacy indeed; and while for a moment it may appear frightening, on consideration it is found welcome, being, in fact, an archetype of experience. For man is not a person in and by himself, but in and by his relations with other persons, and can be wholly a person only in a total intercourse with another. This total intercourse is an ideal which cannot find anything like its realization among men. It is realizable only when the other party to it is God. Here again Bowman has put his finger on something profound.

THE LIGHT UNAPPROACHABLE

There is yet a further stage. As we meditate on power, wisdom, goodness, and all the attributes which we ascribe to God, and realize more and more that in him they must be present in an absolute degree, so we come to realize that in this absolute degree they are something beyond our conception. Anselm found this as he went on in the *Proslogion*. He began with God as that than which no greater can be conceived, and set himself to work out inside this framework the attributes of God. In doing so he came to the recognition that that than which no greater can be conceived is itself something greater than can be conceived, the greatest thinkable is is too great to be thinkable. This, he says, is the light unapproachable in which God dwells, and nothing other than God can enter into that light and see God in his fullness.[1] It is true, the more we learn about God the more we learn that he is inscrutable, and dwells in a light which is darkness to us. And so the idea of God embodies a striking paradox. He is the Archetype of archetypes, but an archetype which we cannot see. He is the realization of our ideals, in a form which we cannot understand. In so far as the idea of God is drawn from our own purposes and standards, it has meaning; but in so far as he is conceived as absolute, he negates all meaning. All positive statements about him are mere pointers. We must unsay them as fast as we say them. But we can never stop saying them, because to leave them unsaid would be more misleading still.

An ideal is a quality of life which we have potentially and desire to have actually, or which we have in a measure and desire to have wholly. For ourselves, it is an object of desire and effort; but when we see it embodied in someone else we admire it, and are drawn to contemplation and imitation of that person. When we see it embodied in someone in a degree which seems high above our reach, we do more than admire and contemplate and imitate—we are humbled before it, and are drawn to service.

God, as the supreme ideal and synthesis of all ideals, is supremely admirable and supremely attractive. We are drawn to contemplate, to imitate, to worship him. Being higher than all height, he is supremely humbling, and draws us to his service. But can we serve him? Yes, on condition that his will for us is known or knowable; and in so far as

[1] *Proslogion*, chaps. 14–16.

this is so, the identification of ourselves with his will gives us an objectivity of standpoint, and sets free impulses in us which are usually inhibited by the overpowering sense of our own weakness. Its fruits are thus strength, unity, and wisdom. But at the same time we know that God is beyond us, and his will is beyond our conceiving. Can we even contemplate him truly, without weaving our own fantasies which will become idols and get between him and us? Can we know enough of his will to serve him truly, and not build fantastic structures of our own which will be only Towers of Babel? Who are we that darken counsel by words without knowledge? We are senseless as the beasts and worthless as dust and ashes before him.

The Christian life is a continued alternation and interpenetration of these two attitudes.

WAYS OF KNOWING GOD

This tension between knowledge and ignorance of God brings to the fore an issue which has hitherto been passed over, but which now demands attention. The idea of God has been built up from a single foundation, namely the human mind or spirit, conscious of its own finitude and imperfection, but drawn to project its own highest qualities to infinity and to seek them at the centre of reality. From this starting-point we have proceeded along two parallel roads: on the one hand arguing to God as the purposive controller of history, who enters into personal intercourse with us, and on the other hand building up the idea of him out of our ideals, raised to an absolute level. Both these processes of thought are at work in Christianity, and it is clear that as they go on they will interpret and support one another. For in the first place it is clear that unless we begin with some idea of God and his character, and so of what he may be expected to want of us, no situation that can arise will bear any meaning for us, and the line of communication between him and ourselves cannot be set up. On the other hand, it is equally clear that as we go on our way under his guidance our understanding of life will alter and our ideals undergo modification, and this will react upon our conception of God. So far we have taken for granted that it is possible for us to do our thinking about God in this double way. But now a problem has arisen which puts it in serious doubt; for God in his capacity as Archetype of archetypes has retired beyond the range of our knowledge, and if he remains there the key to our interpretation of situations as they arise will be taken away.

Our first thought in these circumstances is to ask whether there is any other way in which our knowledge of God might be supplemented and clarified. Three possibilities alone exist, and we must consider them in order.

POSSIBLE SOURCES OF KNOWLEDGE

Nature

We have already held that God shows himself in the situations which arise in our daily life: but is he not also to be found in speculative inference based on the general structure of our universe? It used to be held that the fundamental principles of science were such as to involve him as a necessary consequence. This is no longer true; but yet, when we have accepted him on our own grounds, and are thus committed to regarding the universe as his work, may it not lend itself to decipherment on something like the old lines and yield, even now, a kind of philosophical theism? Do not the heavens still declare his glory?

The heavens declare his glory only to those who already believe in him. Even to these they do not tell anything new, they only illustrate the truths which they already have and invest them with a strong emotional aura; which is a good thing from the point of view of devotion, but not from our present point of view. We cannot find in the physical world more of God than we already know from other sources.

"Mystical" Contemplation

Some wish to escape from this frustration by rising into a new mode of apprehension, higher and truer than the senses and discursive thought, a "vision", often called "mystical", which sees behind the veil of sense. Such language may mean much or little. It may mean no more than an intuitive apprehension, such as may come to a poet or a metaphysician, of something which could after all be analysed and expressed discursively by anyone who had the patience to do it. In that case it is nothing to get excited about. Or it may mean that mode of contemplation, well known in all or most of the higher religions, which puts all definite images and ideas beneath the "cloud of forgetting", and approaches God in the "cloud of unknowing". This is a real way of approach to God, and in itself perfectly normal and healthy, but it is no solution of our problem. Rather it is the very problem itself, namely that in order to approach God we have at a certain point to leave the human understanding behind.

It may be urged that the cloud is darkness only to the discursive intellect, which it defeats, whereas in itself it is light. This may in a sense be true, but still it only changes the shape of our problem. For then we have to point out that no one except a recluse can spend his life in this cloud, be it of light or of darkness. The ordinary man spends his life in the world, thinking and speaking and acting. Then either his contemplative life is to be cut off from his active life, which means that he will be a divided personality, or the former must be brought to bear upon the latter. And how can it, unless it is translated into terms which the discursive intellect can grasp? And again, how can that be? Our problem remains.

Revelation

We might be secured at least against grievous error and set on the right way if God himself would speak, not in the way in which he continually speaks, by merely marshalling events, but by communicating a message couched in human terms, in words and concepts, which we could then use with confidence as our clue to the interpretation of events. No doubt God would have to speak so as to be understood by us, i.e. in the language known to us, and therefore in images and abstract terms such as we ourselves use; but he could presumably do what is wholly beyond our power, namely furnish a set of images and concepts which were guaranteed free from harmful error, and could be used as a standard for our own thinking thereafter. This is the idea of *revelation*.

Christianity affirms that God has actually done this, the recipients of the revelation being first a nation chosen out for the purpose, and then smaller groups within that nation who became the bearers of deeper truths. But Christianity affirms also that God has done more than this. He has appeared in person and lived among us as one of us. In so doing he showed his mind and character in the form of a human life, while at the same time, in his public and private utterances, laying down in conceptual terms the standard for its interpretation. This overcomes our difficulty as far as is at all possible by giving a full revelation in a single human life-span.

Is this a thing which could have been known independently by human "reason"? The historical fact of the Incarnation is evidently not so. Historical facts can only be known empirically. But that is not the whole story. Facts do not manifest themselves to us of their own motion, without our doing anything to help. If the facts give us sensory evidence of their occurrence it is we who, by applying concepts to the interpretation of the sensory evidence, find meaning in it and so become aware of the facts. No facts can be recognized for what they are unless, in addition to being presented to us by the senses, they meet in us an idea which can interpret them. The idea may first arise in us on the occasion of the facts being presented to us, or it may have been framed by us beforehand; as the idea of Neptune was in Adams' mind before he saw the planet. Now, in the present instance it is a mere matter of history that a complex mass of ideas had come into existence, and become almost world wide, before the revealing act of God was performed; and that in performing it he fulfilled widespread expectations and made use of images and concepts that go back to the earliest ages of man. The idea of God himself; of revelation by dream, by inspiration, by theophany, by incarnation; of the divine king who dies for his people; of sacrifice, atonement, and rebirth; these and many more

45

pre-existing ideas constitute the framework in which the Incarnation actually took place. We had thought of it before God did it.

The relation between the idea and the facts is indeed reciprocal. The idea illuminates the facts and is itself accredited by finding facts to illuminate. At the same time it is noteworthy that the fact, when it really happens, in great measure corrects and alters our preconception. Christ is the Jewish hope, perhaps, but not at all as the Jews had held it; yet it is strange that the new form which he gives it is actually more adequate and true to its underlying intention than the current formulations were. His relation to the Gentile hope is just the same. And as the idea interprets the facts while submitting to correction by them, so each confirms and accredits the other. The idea was in the first instance an anticipation built up in faith on the basis of the metaphysical presupposition. Granted that presupposition, and the theism which is its most adequate embodiment, and also the existing state of man, we put these things together and infer revelation and the rest. The initial theism and the presupposition behind it are verified or post-justified when the revelation appears in fact. And it accredits itself as fact by its circumstantiality, fuller of detail (all relevant) than any of the anticipations, and by its completeness as fulfilling them all.

6

Redemption

In the concluding section of the preceding chapter we indicated some of the anticipations which Christ fulfils. In these we included more than the idea of revelation; in addition to this we included ideas which belong to the sphere of redemption. It is time now to pick up this thread, too, and see what facts of experience, when brought into relation with a religious or metaphysical presupposition, give rise to the cycle of ideas which centres on this hope.

The facts are, of course, the familiar ones of evil in life, and the hope of relief is grounded in the inference which we noted earlier as the basis of all eschatology; if God is God, the facts of our present life are not the final facts. Again, we argued that the word which God speaks to us in historical situations must be implicitly a word of promise. If he then goes so far as to speak to us more directly by revelation, it is natural that this word, too, should include a promise and be backed by a deed. What would the promise and the deed have to be?

THE TRAGIC ELEMENT IN LIFE

Man is a maker, a civilizer, always building an ordered world of his own inside nature, and always liable to have it overthrown by forces beyond his control. Such may be the forces of nature herself, operating simply as death-dealing accident—famine, earthquake, disease, and the like. Or they may include the forces of human nature, psychological and social forces, which work deep down below the conscious level and whose behaviour is therefore unpredictable and uncontrollable. These forces may at one time range themselves with the culture-building intelligence and give it creative power, but at another time they may turn against it in a tangle of destructive passions. Cultures and societies then perish from internal causes. It must be largely, though not wholly, to such causes that we should ascribe the most subtle and discouraging malady from which human life can suffer—the tendency of human actions to turn round upon themselves and bring about the reverse of what they are meant to effect. Goodness, against its proper nature, brings forth evil, and right choices lead us into wrong actions. Man's consciousness of this danger has nowhere found fuller expression than in the poets, especially in tragedy, and from them I shall take examples of what I mean.

It can happen, if fate wills it so, that our best qualities become our ruin, and the good man dies because of what is good in him. Homer's Achilles has this fate: he may live long in inglorious ease or become a good and great man (by Homeric standards) at the cost of dying young. We approve the choice he makes in this situation, but we cannot approve the situation itself. Shakespeare knows something of the same kind in the moral sphere; the best things in us may, in some circumstances, be the causes of our ruin or corruption. Macbeth's vivid imagination betrays him to the tempter, and Othello's trustfulness puts him at the mercy of Iago. Situations of this kind, where the good turns round and destroys us, are a desperate problem for morality and religion. I call them tragic situations, because it is the poets who have faced them most boldly, and in poetry they necessarily take the form of tragedy. Philosophy, I regret to say, too often shuts its eyes or pretends that somehow all is well.

There is another type of tragic situation, worse than this, where the very act by which we mean to do right puts us in the wrong. This may happen through a conflict of duties, as it happens to Orestes in the Trilogy, or to Antigone in the play that bears her name. Or it may happen through accidental ignorance, as in the case of Oedipus—not Freud's Oedipus, but the Oedipus depicted by Sophocles, who does all his unhappy deeds in the process of trying to avoid them or to do something else. Warned by an oracle that he is to bring disaster on his parents, he runs from Corinth to avoid them, and unknowingly runs straight into them at Thebes; he tries to do justice by cursing the unknown murderers of Laius, and the curse comes upon himself; everyone who tries to help him pushes him further into the pit. In the end, without apparently having gained anything in wisdom or virtue to justify his tribulations, irrationally as ever, he is taken into the favour of heaven, and his dead body is sacred. The moral of his story is that however we may wish to do the will of God, we cannot, because facts over which we have no control have settled it otherwise. We are morally impotent, the sport of impersonal forces which turn our actions round against themselves and fulfil the opposite of our intentions.

This Oedipus is not a mere fable; his trouble is that of all mankind. Our own generation has had to learn anew the ambivalence of human actions, whereby the very deed which is meant to remedy an evil sets another in its place, or the doing of good brings evil with it. And here again we have something which the philosophers have not always faced. But the poet Sophocles knew it, and his verdict was that "the best thing of all is, never to be born". Modern philosophy, in the persons of Hegel and Marx, has pretended to recognize the facts, but has twisted them into the shape of a dialectic which leads to an ultimate solution. There are no lasting solutions in real life, only perpetual tensions between the good will and the claims which it has to meet or the facts upon which it has to work.

No one feels the pinch of tragedy more than the would-be servant of God. To the mere humanist, trying to build up a decent pattern of life, it is bad enough, but to the believer in God it is the frustration of higher ambitions than that. It is in his mind to dedicate all his actions to the service of God; and since God is the ideal and above the ideal, he can properly be served only by an act, or rather a lifelong series of acts, altogether good and infinitely significant. Such an act, or such a life, and only that, would be a fitting tribute to God. Even if we could do this we should still have to confess ourselves, in the words of the Gospel, "useless slaves" who "have merely done what we ought". But in fact we find ourselves ignorant, impotent, subject to tragic fate, and the service which we try to render to God is beyond our power. By being what he is he sets us an infinite task; and by letting the world be what it is he makes the task doubly impossible.

IS THERE A WAY OUT OF THE IMPASSE?

Is there any way out of this impasse? One way which is sometimes attempted is that of withdrawal into another world, a plane of life and action on which the tragic problems do not arise. This is the hope of the pietist, the sectarian, the purist, who tries to avoid guilt by avoiding responsibility, and is therefore driven in varying degrees to sever himself from society or even to abstain from active life, cultivating an inner life in himself. But it is impossible thus to avoid responsibility. Abstention from action is itself an action, and withdrawal from society has social consequences. The purist, by the very fact of keeping aloof, incurs that guilt which is the reverse side of his fancied innocence, and so runs into a tragic situation of his own.

Perhaps it may be said that tragic situations are a mark of social immaturity, and can therefore be progressively removed by the improvement of social institutions. But while some such situations are certainly amenable to this treatment (Orestes's dilemma could not occur in that form after the suppression of the blood feud), the history of human institutions strongly suggests that the removal of one set of conflicts does no more than set the stage for others. But perhaps, again, this is due to the continuing presence of ill will or sin in our midst, and the way out of tragedy will be found in the eradication of sin or (to put it in more modern terms) in the continuing moral progress of mankind. This may be so, but it is cold comfort for those who have to live in the sinful world that now is, and who see how far mankind is from making any detectable progress in the abolition of sin. Besides, it is not certain that the evil of tragedy does arise wholly from sin, though, of course, the tragic situation can be made still worse by the ways in which sinful men react to it. But it seems to be inherent in finitude and the ignorance and weakness which go with it. Its roots grow not in the human will as such, but in the very foundations of the universe. That is why the Greeks ascribed it to an impersonal fate, to which even the gods were subject.

GOD ALONE CAN SUPPLY THE ANSWER AND HAS DONE SO

How can man be delivered from this world of death? Only if he can put himself under another government, if Fate can give place to Providence. In the long run the question what God means by asking the impossible, or by letting good become a source of evil, can be answered only by God, and it is he who must reveal the right way to approach these things.

Christianity affirms that he has done so in the history of Israel and the Church. Here he has inserted into history a divinely guided community which embodies and diffuses that form of life which is his real purpose for us.

The idea of a life singled out from the general run of the world and placed under the special providence of God meets us first in the story of Abraham. His whole life is built on a promise, and the promise is that his children shall become a nation under God's special protection. God undertakes to build up a community, called into existence by his special act, with its Law ordained by him to shape its life and character in the proper direction. The life of Israel is to be richly blessed. It is to be the good life itself, not laboriously achieved by man, but freely given by God. Or so it seems. Yet Israel's history is one of continual failure to act or even to hope rightly. The fundamental tragic tensions appear in Israel as well as outside it, and are not resolved or transcended. Priesthood and prophecy come to be and remain at odds. The sabbatical law, Israel's glory, is a political and military menace.

Misconceived as to its purpose and function, the whole Law nourishes national pride and exclusiveness while inhibiting the growth of a free culture. Precept conflicts with precept and justice with mercy. Job and Ecclesiastes are written and published, and the pessimism of the latter can compare with that of the pagan Sophocles. "I praised the dead which are already dead more than the living which are yet alive; yea, better than both did I esteem him which hath not yet been, who hath not seen the evil work that is done under the sun." Why then, we may ask, has Ecclesiastes a pious ending and Job a happy one? Was Israel also running away from the naked fact of tragedy? And for us, what is the moral of the coming of tragedy to Israel? Simply, I think, that the problem cannot be dealt with by a mere re-ordering of life on this plane. Messiah must come from heaven and bring the New Jerusalem, which is in heaven; the evil of life can only be corrected by bringing in a new dimension.

The new dimension must be brought in without the old one being removed. It is no solution to escape from earth into heaven and live a life, hidden in God, which makes no impact here. The Kingdom is not of this world, but it must be active in this world and give its citizens a quality of life in which tragedy is overcome. It must be in this world, with power and significance that overcome the tragedy of this world. And this, as the fate of Israel warns us, cannot be done simply by good legislation and moral instruction. Tragedy is in the build of things. The Kingdom must overcome it in the only way left open, by taking it up into itself and transfiguring it. The tragic situation must be accepted and robbed of its sting.

To bring the problem to a point: God's will is above all that we can see or do, and yet we want, while remaining men, to become its organs. We need so to act in a tragic situation as, by accepting it, to rise above it into the freedom of God. Our act must have freedom and significance, not by being rid of its limitations, but because of and in and through them. But this is only possible if God himself gives a human act this power.

God the Son has done so, according to the Christian story, by performing the act himself. He takes upon himself limitation, not merely enduring it, but choosing it; being God, he becomes man, and as man he lives at first in poverty and insignificance. When he enters upon his public career every good thing in him and around him is turned to his destruction. His virtue, which should attract men and does attract some, provokes in others the hostility which ends in his death. His life has to be lived and his teaching given in forms which lay themselves open to manifold and radical misunderstanding. At last he dies by violence, a painful death, accompanied by public disgrace, unjustly inflicted, with the mockery of a trial, and the highest religious tribunal of God's own people sentences God to death for blasphemy because he has said who he is. Finally, on the cross itself, the innocent sufferer meets the ultimate dereliction of all, and feels himself abandoned by the Father to whom even Job in the story had not appealed in vain. Yet, while thus feeling in his own life the fullest weight of tragedy, he makes every incident of it an act of ready obedience to the Father, and so sets an example of creative and victorious suffering.

This is not all. If it were, he would still be no more than a nobler Socrates. He would have shown us how to perish nobly, but he would still have perished and left us to perish. But by thus obeying and submitting to the very end he wins the right and the power to rise from the grave in glory, and to enter on a new life beyond the sphere of tragedy and other evils altogether. He is still a human individual, still clothed in a recognizable human body, but now he is free to move at will through time and space, and is henceforth active everywhere with the full power of his Godhead. He has lifted humanity, in his own Person, on to a different plane of existence, and our humanity is exalted with his in so far as we become members incorporate in his mystical body. To this end he has set up the Church, with teachings and practices deriving from himself, expressing in word and action the nature of the true life which God intends for us, and with supernatural powers to impart and sustain it. Moulded by these influences we come progressively to share Christ's mind, to act and suffer like him; and as we do so our actions and sufferings become, as it were, incorporated with his, and become parts of the one full, perfect, and sufficient sacrifice and oblation; the act of homage offered to God by the only competent Agent, whose worth and significance are without limit.

We ourselves, limited on earth, are henceforward free and powerful in heaven, and this our power works, beyond what we ourselves know, for the redemption of all mankind. But the results are partly visible even now in our changed relationships with other people; for when we pray in the person of Christ there is no limitation upon our prayer, such as there would be if it merely expressed our own desires. Prayer that is only the pouring out of our own desires is limited and spoiled by our ignorance and ill will. It is then that prayers can conflict, and God's petitioners appear before him flourishing a whole array of claims and counter-claims. But prayer in the person of Christ and in the power of the Spirit is prayer for the fulfilment of the work of Christ; all details, if we care to mention any, are meant simply as instances and illustrations of that, and if he fulfils his work in ways which we did not expect or desire, we gladly accept the result, provided that his work is really done. And since we are full of ignorance and evil, and since the risen Christ is active everywhere and always on behalf of all that is good and against all that is evil, we are all the time implicitly praying against something in ourselves and for something in our opponents. In prayer we stand, as in action we cannot, above the limitations from which the opposition springs. Knowing him, moreover, we are knit together in an increasingly real community, even with those whom we do not understand or approve. This does not put an end to disagreement or even to conflict; but it does take the malice out of them, since Christians, even when opposing one another most strongly, can see in one another the friends of God, and so be aware of a fundamental unity. Not only Christians, but often others, too, can be caught up into this unity.

Christianity is so presented by some of its exponents to-day that many people think it offers nothing worth having. One who had grasped imaginatively what has been said might rather feel that it is too good to be true. And yet a more detailed examination of Christianity might lead even such a one to a certain disillusionment. For while it does offer freedom and power, it is a power to do and avoid things of a different order from much that is held worthy of pursuit or avoidance in this world. If we talk of knowledge and power, while offering a kind of knowledge which people have now long since despaired of, and remaining visibly unable either to command prosperity or to secure justice, we shall seem to talk paradoxes at the best and nonsense at the worst. And the only way to meet this obstacle is by frontal attack. People must be told, for it is a central point of Christianity, that their present values are wrong, not merely those which they themselves recognize to be self-centred, but even those of which they are really proud, and that neither in this world nor in Christianity can these be realized at all. Christianity does not exist to satisfy them as they stand, but to correct them; abolishing some, reforming the conception of others, and bringing to life new desires and insights of duty which were not there before. We can say that the Christian life which results from this is a life preferable in quality to any other that man can live, a life of knowledge and freedom; but it is a new life and in some ways a strange one, too.

The change from ordinary ways of looking at things to the Christian way is described in the New Testament by no less violent a metaphor than that of death. We are to deny our present selves, to become dead to the world, to live only with Christ in God. What we shall be is so unlike what we are that at present we cannot really conceive it. This is true even of the Christian himself while still *in via*; it is even more true of the outsider. And this is a side of our message which is not always made clear. We talk of Christianity as solving the world's problems, but we do not talk of it as turning the world upside down. The amount of sheer renunciation that it requires is minimized. And yet it finds expression in the Bible, in the challenging figure of Job, not to say in the supreme challenge of the cross. "Though he slay me, yet will I trust in him" is a fine thing to say when we do not think he really will slay us; but the real doctrine is that, in the mystical sense, and sometimes even in the plain physical sense, that is just what he will do.

No one can receive the Christian life in its true form who has not been through the Christian death. No one can understand the meaning of the good news in Christ who has not willingly abandoned all hope of good news among the potsherds of Job. Between the natural man, who thinks he has claims on the world and arraigns God for not meeting them, and the Christian, who praises God for his astonishing generosity, lies the death of the first man's claims. The case against God, on the natural man's grounds, is unanswerable. We make fools of ourselves if we try to answer it. It is God who must answer the natural man, not by meeting his case, but by leading him to mortify in himself the grounds on which it rested. When we have thus abandoned ourselves and our notions of life, and thrown the whole away as rubbish in the presence of God, and stand naked to receive whatever he gives for the sake of God who gives it, then we find to our surprise that, besides killing us, he also makes us alive, and that his generosity exceeds what we could ever have dreamed of. But it remains generosity in a strange coin.